Praise for David J. Danelo's
The Return

"Because every person's war experience is unique, so is their return home. The combat veterans' reintegration to the society they left is a journey that's been made by returning warriors since before Homer first chronicled it. In this illuminating book, David Danelo provides a worthy perspective for making sense of a largely incommunicable journey and how he came to reconcile the polarities of coming home."

— General James N. Mattis, USMC (ret.)

"*The Return* is the only book I've ever read that compelled me to keep reading... but to go as slowly as possible to savor and ponder each word. Written with the skill and precision of a philosophical sniper who stays awake for days, Danelo looks for one chance to expand your views on war, peace and a soldier's most difficult mission in life—returning to civilian life with people who don't really understand what he went through."

— Matt Furey, author. *The Unbeatable Man*

D1516292

"A wonderfully profound treatment of the veteran's Odyssey."

— Dr. Mackubin Thomas Owens,
national security professor, Naval War College,
and USMC Vietnam veteran

"U.S. Army Green Berets were the first in and last out of the longest war in American History. This book is showing them how to come home and find peace."

— Lieutenant Colonel David Scott Mann
(U.S. Army, Ret.), Green Beret Foundation

"Veterans ask the rest of us to witness and to get it. Witnessing means opening our minds and hearts to their stories with compassion and willingness. Getting it means not judging or attributing pathology, but deeply comprehending the transformations that military service and war inevitably bring to the warrior. David Danelo's *The Return* offers brilliant, moving and accurate witness, presented in powerful and digestible units, to the positive and meaningful transformations that occur as a result of becoming a warrior. He guides fellow veterans in learning how to transform their changes and challenges into strength, gifts and wisdom that benefit us all. And he courageously and honestly shares how he has successfully walked this spiritual warrior's journey to war and back again."

— Edward Tick, Ph.D.; Director, Soldier's Heart, Inc.;
author: *War and the Soul* and *Warrior's Return*

THE
RETURN

DAVID J. DANELO

THE RETURN

A FIELD MANUAL FOR LIFE AFTER COMBAT

DAVID J. DANELO

Black Irish Entertainment LLC

NEW YORK   LOS ANGELES

BLACK IRISH ENTERTAINMENT LLC
ANSONIA STATION
POST OFFICE BOX 237203
NEW YORK, NY 10023-7203

COPYRIGHT © 2014 DAVID J. DANELO
COVER PHOTO COURTESY OF GREGORY MISTLER
COVER DESIGN BY DERICK TSAI, MAGNUS REX
EDITED BY SHAWN COYNE

FIRST BLACK IRISH ENTERTAINMENT
EDITION NOVEMBER 2014

FOR INFORMATION ABOUT SPECIAL DISCOUNTS
FOR BULK PURCHASES,
PLEASE VISIT WWW.BLACKIRISHBOOKS.COM

ISBN: 978-1-936891-31-3
EBOOK ISBN: 978-1-936891-33-7

PRINTED IN THE UNITED STATES OF AMERICA

1   2   3   4   5   6   7   8   9   10

for my brother Matt,
and for those we welcome home

Table of Contents

INTRODUCTION

Since leaving the Marines a decade ago, I've had fun collecting awkward little reminders that fighting in a war is an experience not shared by most people.

On my first day of graduate school, an earnest young professor gazed out at the class and proclaimed: "This will be the most transformative two years of your life."

Minutes after delivering our daughter, the doctor looked up to me and said, in an apparent attempt at reassurance, "I bet you've never seen this much blood before."

Before a morning flight the gate agent invited military service members in uniform to board the plane ahead of elderly passengers and a mother traveling alone with two small kids. As a private fresh from boot camp moved through the clapping crowd, I wondered how many other vets were camouflaged there, uncomfortable with this spectacle of a society's gratitude gone awry.

Each of these brief moments contributed to my own "Exile," as Dave Danelo calls that unsettling sense of being back but not really being home.

Our society has long recognized the challenge of this transition. In his second Inaugural Address, just a month before the Civil War ended, President Lincoln laid out a path of reconciliation for the nation: "Let us strive on to finish the work we are in, to bind up the nation's wounds, *to care for him who shall have borne the battle and for his widow, and his orphan...*" That line, and worthy sentiment, became the motto of the Department of Veterans Affairs. But vets don't come home to federal agencies.

Since 2001, lampposts and bumpers across America have been festooned with yellow ribbons, visible signs of support for all those fighting the nation's wars. Again, a noble sentiment. But vets don't even come home to communities.

We come home to ourselves.

Military units, especially combat units, are characterized by teamwork, camaraderie, and shared purpose. But post-service life—even when filled with family, friends, and colleagues—often brings a solitude made more intense when contrasted with what came before. War changes warriors, as Dave tells us, and the experience of killing for your country—for ten seconds or ten years—never quite fits in with the rest of your life.

Coming home is hard. And to come home, each of us needs to find his or her own way to hold onto all the things that were good about serving, reach resolution with what was not, and help our comrades do the same. Life goes on, and so must we. As Ralph Waldo Emerson said in his essay *Self-Reliance*, "Nothing can bring you peace but yourself."

The Return is a guide to doing just that.

Nathaniel Fick
June, 2014

What we call the beginning is often the end
And to make and end is to make a beginning.
The end is where we start from.

– T. S. Eliot, Four Quartets

PROLOGUE

In April 2004, as a U.S. Marine Corps captain, I was wounded in an insurgent mortar strike while commanding a traffic checkpoint during what is now called the First Battle of Fallujah. Shrapnel struck my left jaw, an inch from a major artery. Although I was treated and returned to duty the next day, two metal fragments remained lodged close to several nerve endings. According to the doctor, attempting to remove the shrapnel could result in further damage. I left them alone.

Over several years, the smallest piece dissolved into tiny slivers that occasionally worked their way out, protruding beyond my skin like any normal scab. The large shard, about a quarter inch long, remains embedded in my chin. My left eyelid twitches slightly from the shrapnel, and sometimes after a long laugh, I still feel a sharp twinge in my jaw. The metal presses back on the scar tissue whenever my young daughter presses her little fingers to my face in exploration, or my Italian father reflexively pinches my cheeks following a vigorous embrace.

Back in 2004, as combat operations continued in and around Fallujah, my interaction with the amorphous war led me to two irreconcilable personal conclusions. First, I enjoyed my work and was good at it. During peacetime, I was an average officer at best, but I had trained for over a decade to lead in combat. For whatever reason, Iraq's moral abstractions made sense to me. By every metric I could rationally assess, I thrived in counterinsurgency's chaotic rhythm.

At the same time, my instincts—those fusions of logic and gut we all grow to depend on as our inner compass—told me I should leave the military. I had joined a decade before the war started, attending the U.S. Naval Academy in the 1990s, well before events following the 9/11 attacks created an aura of glamour around military service. When I swore my oath of office in the summer of 1994, military service was not fashionable. My college-bound friends didn't scorn my choice to prostrate my youth upon the Naval Academy's unforgiving martial altar, but nobody felt compelled to praise me either.

Before the Iraq War started, I had planned to leave the military. I had earned a scholarship to a dual graduate degree program in environmental science and engineering; alternative energy seemed a promising profession. But when war called, I extended my active duty time and, instead of leaving, volunteered to fight. The opportunity for combat sated a deeply personal desire—an experience which was, in and of itself, far more meaningful than the obligatory "thank you for your service" civilian family and friends all too hastily proffered. *I didn't do it for you*, I wanted to say when a new acquaintance gushed over my profession. *I did it for me.*

Part of why I joined the military was to feel as though I had earned my freedom, at least in my own eyes. But satisfying that sentiment didn't solve the puzzle of what I should do with my liberty once it was attained. What civilian profession could match the thrill of pitting my judgment, analysis, and instinct against forces out to destroy me and my team? What work environment could tap into the warrior's sixth sense that mystically appeared when cosmic adrenaline aligned with technical skill? What words would a human resources director understand that could describe the same type of satisfaction? What else was I born to do?

As I pondered this in Iraq, I remembered a mentor's wisdom. "You can only leave the Marine Corps in three ways," the officer had said. "They tell you to leave. You decide to go. Or you die fighting." Setting aside the valor option, ending active duty on the military's terms seemed like the worst choice. After all, why fight a war if I have no intention of enjoying a life of peace? What's the point in protecting freedom if I never partake in the liberty I've pledged my life to defend? What does my service mean if I have no connection with the citizens who sleep safely because I stand ready to strike those who would harm them?

Shortly before my shrapnel encounter, I had developed an email correspondence with a professional writer whose work challenged, inspired, and motivated me. His complimentary suggestion that I might have literary potential felt like Michael Jordan saying I played good basketball. I resolved to give it a shot—in part because I thought working for myself might be the only thing that could match combat's challenge and exhilaration. I wanted a civilian job as demanding and fulfilling as the warrior path. If freelance writing wasn't hard, what was?

From tech start-ups to taco stands, first-time businesses have an extraordinarily high casualty rate. On average, ninety-five percent of all entrepreneurial ventures fail within the first five years. Over half die in the first year. When I left the Marines, I received a lot of conservative suggestions from well-meaning advisors. *Develop your start-up while maintaining a secure job. Stockpile a year of living expenses before plunging in. Have a backup plan in case your dream doesn't work out.*

While these are good principles, entrepreneurship by its very nature—not unlike combat— requires an enthusiasm for risk that can border on insanity. By pushing on with the crazy notion of independence, I had volunteered, like any entrepreneur, for my own personal economic hunger games. Did I really think I had what it took to be the one in twenty left standing? Did I really believe my skills could offer me security apart from Big Employer?

Yes. As a combat veteran, that's exactly what I believed. My business model wasn't too keen, but I thought I could improvise, adapt, and overcome my way into making it profitable. After all, I had been tested under fire with comrades who had fought and won on the streets of Fallujah. I had disciplined, trained, endured, blossomed, and survived. I told myself that I had seen and done more than ninety-nine percent of my civilian competitors. And I believed that made me better.

I was more than a little naïve. Looking back now on a decade of solo adventures, I'm aware that the confidence I felt could just as easily have been misplaced. War may produce fleeting moments of nobility and honor in one's character, but combat does not make a person more or less likely to competently avoid capitalism's pitfalls or responsibly navigate a freedom-filled life. Does war deepen life experience? Definitely. Does that guarantee entrepreneurial success? Not by a long shot.

Outside of my professional life, I was also trying to discover that elusive "community" where every transitioning warrior is told to find refuge. I visited the Veterans for Foreign Wars and American Legion halls. I joined the local volunteer fire department. I linked up with veterans groups online.

None of them filled the void. Community seemed like an imaginary abstraction, not real people. If a community for veterans like me was out there, I couldn't find it. Ultimately, I could not escape the haunting awareness that my warrior identity did not fit with "normal," whatever that was.

The first couple of years I was writing, I also went through what I would now describe as ordinary transition issues. One time, I had an idea for a side job as a fitness instructor that included formation runs at 0630 (yes, in the morning) through a residential neighborhood. When someone pointed out that children might be sleeping, I snapped. *Who are those people to think they are worthy of rest? What about the warriors who are fighting for their freedom? What are we doing for them?*

Things never got too bad, at least not in comparison to some of my comrades. My strange combat-related dreams stopped after a couple of years, as did the jumpiness and twitching when doors slammed. Sometime in late 2005, I was no longer swerving under overpasses. By Independence Day 2006, I could handle fireworks. The explosive anger that often appeared for no particular reason seemed more manageable. I went back to Iraq as a writer and got shot at for the first time without carrying a weapon. The familiarity felt oddly comfortable.

As I had hoped, my combat experiences had become useful in my chosen profession. One book was published, then another. Speaking gigs and consulting contracts materialized. Clients started seeking me out. Debts that had accumulated during the start-up years dwindled and then finally disappeared. Through calculated risk, prudent perseverance, and mysterious luck, I stumbled into something that looked like success. Somehow my gamble had actually worked. I had transitioned. At least that was what everyone told me.

Even as I was making the transition into… something…many warriors I had bonded with and fiercely cared about were going in a different direction. They had nasty addictions, awful jobs, disastrous relationships and unhappy lives. They had no idea how to put their combat adrenaline to productive use. They called me and we talked. It was what their counselors and therapists told them to do. I still take these calls, sometimes from people I haven't spoken to in years.

Every time I listened to stories from my brave and broken friends, I left the conversation feeling guilty that I had not done enough. And my own process did not sound like what therapists and counselors were telling them to do. Why was I moving forward with my life even without the community I was supposed to have? Why was I relatively content as a civilian while others—who suffered through the same struggles—felt devastated, depressed and destroyed? Why were some of these warriors strong while others were suicidal? Why was I somewhat okay and they were not?

I started talking with Vietnam veterans about their transitions. I read books like Jonathan Shay's *Odysseus in America* and Karl Marlantes' *What it is Like to Go to War*. I thought about my father's father, who returned from World War II and, as my dad described, "just didn't talk about it." I wondered what those who made it back home from previous wars had in common with my comrades and me. In what ways were we similar to past generations who went on to live as civilians with enthusiasm, meaning, and purpose? And how were we different?

I started questioning much of the conventional wisdom. Is post-traumatic stress really a disorder? Or is it a normal, natural human response to the shock of coming from war to peace? Do we really need communities of like-minded veterans to develop the resilient spirits we know are necessary to become the people we want to be? If counseling and therapy are supposed to be effective, then why do many of my Marines say they feel worse after their sessions? Is there anything I am thinking or doing that others are not?

As my writing and research career evolved, I still didn't feel like I fit in anywhere. But I had stopped thinking I was supposed to. I had assembled a motley crew of my own military and civilian comrades—

trusted friends who, even if they hadn't been there, could empathize with war and veterans who had seen the fiercest combat and still embraced the quiet pleasures of peace.

I found myself most inspired by those who, no matter their background, seemed to be at home in both peace and war. Some found community; some did not. Some were religious; others were not. Some kept in contact with combat comrades; others avoided anything warlike. They had all types of families and diverse personal relationships. But the ones who made it back home all seemed to have one thing in common—they had not just transitioned. They had returned.

Transitioning is structural. Transitioning is about taking skills and aptitudes and repurposing them from one type of economic endeavor into another. It is important to transition, but it is not enough. To return is to complete a spiritual rite of passage; a psychic cycle; a heroic journey. Those who return can go back and forth in various mental and emotional places, all the while being grounded in who they are. They have evolved. They can walk comfortably in opposite worlds.

This constant rhythm of returning is the method, logic, and process I have applied toward my own challenges and, in some way, what I'm still trying to do every day. Returning has become my compass point—something I attempt to accomplish through awareness of the ironies, paradoxes, and dualities I have seen in both war and peace. Returning is how I found my new normal.

What follows is a woodpile of ideas that has fueled the fires of my mind, heart, and spirit for the past decade. There are large logs in here for heavy heat, and some small kindling for getting started. If you are trying to return, or trying to help someone get there, I hope this stack of sticks will help. Take anything that is beneficial, and leave whatever is not behind. And most important—for all of us—do whatever it takes to keep your flame burning.

PART ONE

EXILE

1

WHAT IS EXILE?

Have you ever achieved a difficult goal? Lost a hundred pounds in a year? Placed first in the shooting competition? Birthed children? Sent them to college? Finished a dissertation? Won the championship? Nailed the big proposal? Closed on the dream house? Finally heard her say yes?

Returning from combat in a foreign land—taking off the warrior's uniform and coming back as a civilian—is an achievement that should theoretically culminate in euphoria. It's supposed to be a triumphant feeling—the victorious end of a long journey. What happens instead? As soon as you're back, you wish you had never returned.

You had worked for years to get where you were. Your family and friends watched and cheered. They saw the deep meaning and purpose you felt when you finished boot camp. They held you and then cried when you walked toward the plane with your comrades, en route to war.

But now you are back again. Back with your friends; your family; your pets. Back in the village you left, with the same people talking about the same things. You fought the good fight, and you thought you would feel amazing. Instead you are bored, empty, depressed, and hopeless. You're thinking about collecting intelligence on the enemy; dodging rocket propelled grenades and roadside bombs; hunting and killing a fierce, evil foe. They are thinking about what's for dinner. You thought you were progressing. Instead, you are regressing.

"When I was here, I wanted to be there. When I was there, all I could think of was getting back to the jungle," said Martin Sheen's Captain Willard in *Apocalypse Now*.

That is Exile.

2

EXILE AND THE HERO

Almost a century ago, mythologist Joseph Campbell wrote *The Hero with a Thousand Faces*, which argued that all stories—and lives—follow a similar mythical pattern. Whether it is *The Odyssey* or *Pride and Prejudice* or *Star Wars* or *The Girl with the Dragon Tattoo*, Campbell believed these universal story myths, as he called them, represented the same quest for meaning, maturity and mastery. The hero or heroine, Campbell thought, was making an identical journey of departure, adventure, and return in an infinite number of forms.

In any story, mythical or real, the climactic adventure is the most exciting part. The hero trains for a decade to run one hundred meters in the Olympic Games. The heroine works nights on her novel and finally, after twenty-eight rejections, receives a return call from an agent. Rocky Balboa fights Apollo Creed; Gandalf slays the orcs. A warrior sacrifices for honor and country. In this way, the stories we read, hear and watch are all different expressions for lifting ourselves up, finding new experiences, drawing on ancient wisdom, and making ourselves more useful to our families, communities, and countries.

In story and in life, the hardest part of the hero's journey is the return. It's the place where you try to take everything you've learned and make it real, but you feel like no one else understands. It's also the part nobody tunes in to watch. There's nothing exciting about Han Solo grilling on the patio or Gandalf brewing morning coffee. Exile is the trial of silence—the schizophrenia following the thrill.

Can you identify with the feeling of returning to a once-familiar place and feeling dislocated because something has changed you? We have all gone through this before, but it's different and scarier for returning veterans. The thrilling stakes of life and death are now simply choices to make for the life you want to live. How do you make those choices? How do you return from Exile?

3

EXILE IS NORMAL

When I was stationed at Twentynine Palms, a Marine Corps base in California's Mojave Desert, I heard a story about a legendary Native American ritual. In a certain tribe, when young men returned from their first time on the warpath, they were required to spend a full year away from tribal council. They were not permitted to sit amongst the council elders or participate in group decisions. But after their banishment ended, the warrior was welcomed back and seated at a place of honor.

Setting aside the practical questions, (like what happened if a rival tribe attacked during the warrior's year in purgatory) the story's spirit feels true. Exile is the dislocation that tribal exclusion represented. The place of honor back in the tribal council—confident and content with a new life—is the return the warrior seeks.

Although Exile is particularly acute in returning veterans, it isn't restricted to them. Exile is the letdown that follows any triumphant, climactic victory. It is the theoretical happily-ever-after that never arrives. It is an enduring, empty frustration that you've lost the one skill you knew you possessed; the one life you are trying to move on from, but which you can never go back to. And now you don't know where you belong.

New mothers call it the baby blues. Freshly minted PhDs call it dissertation depression. Olympic athletes call it medal mourning. Buzz Aldrin, one of the only humans to walk on the moon, described Exile as "the melancholy of all things done."

"I was petrified of losing the one thing in my mind I was good at," said British swimmer Cassie Patten, talking about her life after the Olympic Games.

Now add up those feelings and quadruple them. This is Exile as veterans confront it.

4

EXILE IS REFUSING TO RETURN

Can we get back to Joseph Campbell for a minute? This hero's journey stuff is important. In his book, Campbell describes the last phase of the hero's journey in three stages.

The first is when the hero refuses to really return. The body may be home, but the mind and heart are still back in the fight. Think of the last scene in *The Hurt Locker*, where Sergeant First Class William James absentmindedly pushes a shopping cart though the supermarket. Consider Luke Skywalker standing outside the campfire circle at the end of *Return of the Jedi*, refusing to join the group lest he soil his wholesome energy. The return seems boring compared to the adventure.

When veterans refuse to return, they tell themselves—as the *Hurt Locker* explosives expert silently did while scanning the cereal aisle—that they have "lost the one thing they really love," and that nothing will ever take its place again. They resign themselves, unnecessarily, to a belief that their best days are behind them, that nothing will ever mean as much as their time in the fight.

The veteran in Exile comes back from the war, grows out his hair, and goes to college. She joins a student committee to inflate her ego with war stories and flaunt her status. He signs on to the local police force or fire department not because he cares about protecting society, but because he doesn't know what else to do. If there's no heroic end for a veteran—no reason they fought the good fight— then there's no point in returning in the first place. This is one reason why so many veterans work for military contractors or security companies. Why go back to civilian life when you can get paid even more to keep fighting?

Returning veterans traumatize their family with anger and aggression because they are unwilling to calm down. They are constantly on watch because complacency kills. And they are forever engaged in heroic fantasies because they hate the thought of becoming nasty, worthless, disgusting, boring civilians again.

5

EVERYONE'S EXILE
IS DIFFERENT

Each combat veteran returns to civilian life having had a different war. Many veterans, depending on the number of their deployments, had three, four, or five different wars. Likewise, every veteran will face his or her own personal Exile as they strive to return. The demons of dislocation are all similar, but the ways they affect returning warriors are as distinctive as DNA. Some are wounded with brain injuries from explosions or gunshots. Some have eerie thoughts that prevent normal feeling, thinking, communicating, sensing and remembering. Some are deeply troubled by either civilian or military life. And some come back without any apparent emotional or psychological trauma.

Some combat veterans feel shame at not having done enough, in their minds, to earn "combat veteran" status. The soldier tells his girlfriend that he only stayed inside the wire and didn't go on any missions. She can't understand why he gets angry when she is happy he wasn't in danger. He didn't want to stay safe; he wanted to prove bravery and courage. He thinks he hasn't done his part.

Every veteran has encountered war along a spectrum—a bell curve or graph representing the violence inflicted upon or done by him and physical courage expressed in choices along the way. On the upper extreme are veterans who sought out combat and received a lot of it. They may have positive or negative feelings about their experience, but they definitely got what they wanted.

On the other end are veterans whose deployments were imposed—who didn't really want to fight and actively avoided risk whenever they had the chance. Ironically, these veterans sometimes tell the loudest stories, seeking to cover their shame with narratives about experiences they never had. Only each veteran really knows—assuming his or her brain retains functional ability.

Most returning warriors fall somewhere in the
middle. They have seen and done more than some
and less than others. They are emotionally dislocated
and confused about their new peaceful environment.
They are in Exile, but not in an unrecoverable way.

6

EXILE IS YOUR ENEMY

One significant distinction between civilians and warriors is the attitude, or mindset, they take toward their opponents. Civilians, especially politicians running campaign commercials, often use moral language to dehumanize their adversary: good versus evil; us versus them; light versus darkness. The enemy is treated as a non-person, worthy only of condemnation, scorn or death.

Warriors, on the other hand, treat their enemy with great respect. In Afghanistan, infantry Marines, patrolling soldiers and Navy SEALs rarely call the Taliban "terrorists." Their opponent knows the terrain, maintains tactical discipline, and ambushes with overwhelming firepower. Warriors know when they are up against skilled professionals and wisely acknowledge their foes as worthy adversaries rather than dismissing them as cowards, cretins or criminals.

As a transitioning veteran, Exile is the foe you must face. The emptiness, displacement and confusion can make you feel as trapped as Jonah in the whale's belly, as starved as Jesus in the desert, and as poor as Job in his lowest trials. Why, God? Why have you forsaken me?

Psychologists and parents sometimes limit Exile's strength by declaring the rootless emotional wandering all transitioning veterans feel is depression or disorder. Like dehumanizing the enemy in combat, these labels might wrongly suggest counseling or medication as a straightforward prescription. When these don't work, warriors wonder what they are doing wrong. Perhaps they have failed to confront the real threat.

Like facing the Taliban, overcoming Exile requires the judgment to recognize the enemy's existence and the awareness to respect its power.

7

EXILE IS FEAR

In his historical fiction epic *Gates of Fire*, novelist Steven Pressfield claims the opposite of fear—spoiler alert—is love. Writing about the Spartans who died to preserve Western civilization at the battle of Thermopylae, Pressfield frames this love as self-sacrifice, fierce devotion and humble passion dedicated to a cause worth dying for.

But what about the inverse question? What is the opposite of love? Is it fear as well? If that is true, then what does fear look like? For returning veterans, fear takes form in Exile.

The warrior culture defines itself, in many ways, as the avoidance of civilian luxury. Consider Chris McCandless, as portrayed in *Into the Wild*, who rejected "things, things, things" as meaningless compared to the purity of testing himself anew each day in Alaska. Although not about war, McCandless' battle against the wilderness depicts a warrior's inner struggle to find meaning and purpose in routine life. Becoming civilians again can be terrifying for warriors who fear losing their souls if they meekly submit to a normal job, suburban routine and daily commute.

Returning warriors have a hard time talking about this fear. Civilians think they fear the enemy, or killing, or death, or memories. Warriors may have feared some or all of these things before combat, but they rarely encounter these fears in the fight. What warriors most fear is shame—failing to perform honorably for their mates. Warriors fear blaspheming their beliefs, and maintaining the martial faith is what keeps them going.

Exile triggers this virulent and primal fear. For many warriors, the ultimate violation of their ethos is becoming a civilian again. The civilian world—the place that values peace, happiness, and calm pursuit of personal dreams—embraces the antithesis of warrior values. In combat, warriors overcome fear by motivating themselves to live up to their peers, leaders and ancestors. Without this inspiration a warrior in Exile is terrified and hollow, lacking a passion, purpose and dream.

8

EXILE CAN KILL

Do you remember Greg Louganis, the American diving champion from the 1984 Los Angeles and 1988 Seoul Summer Olympic Games? Louganis, who is openly gay and HIV positive, has spoken candidly about his struggles with depression following his rise to celebrity and fame. Today, Louganis is a coach, actor, dog agility trainer, and human rights activist. By almost any metric, Louganis has achieved a successful life.

You might not remember Mark Lenzi, who won gold four years later in the 1992 Barcelona Summer Games. Lenzi was the first diver ever to score one hundred points in competition, making him technically superior to Louganis. Returning home to Fredericksburg, Virginia, Lenzi thought his performance would earn him the same widespread social affection Louganis received.

Fame, however, is a fickle mistress—and she did not romance Lenzi for long. "I'm a kid from nowhere and all of a sudden I'm on *The Tonight Show*," Lenzi said in a 1995 interview. "You're being told one day you're a famous athlete, and the next day nobody knows who you are." The Olympian returned to Indiana where he had set diving records but did little more than eat junk food and watch television, adding thirty-five pounds to his lithe frame. Two years later he bounced back, returned to diving, competed in the 1996 Atlanta Olympics and won bronze. He married in 2004 and coached men's and women's diving at East Carolina University from 2009-2011.

Lenzi died on April 9, 2012. He had suffered fainting spells and checked into a hospital, then his blood pressure fell and he never regained consciousness. "There are no words to express how heartfelt a loss this is," said his hero, Greg Louganis. What caused Lenzi's death? We still do not know.

Like warriors who plunge into Exile, Lenzi once climbed to the mountaintop and descended depressed. And if you have ever been overwhelmed with suicidal thoughts, then you might know how it feels to be stripped and exposed before the raw intensity of Exile's tragic, mortal power.

9

EXILE CANNOT BE MEDICATED

Exile and clinical depression are not necessarily the same things. This does not mean some transitioning veterans do not struggle with depression. Many do. But while permanently medicating pain may be good for drug companies, tranquilizing young warriors with Percocet, Prozac, or Paxil will not make Exile go away. Drug dependency makes Exile a time-lapse Grim Reaper, smiling with toothy, triumphal satisfaction as unlimited quantities of pills, joints, and booze destroy lives.

This is a paradox, especially for warriors who have grown comfortable managing combat's highs and lows with Vicodin, Ambien, or Oxytocin. Stimulants and depressants can bring you up and down. What they cannot do is give you ambition. Zoloft may relax, but it doesn't provide meaning, vision and purpose. It cannot motivate you to achieve, evolve or succeed. It won't make fear go away.

Consider Audie Murphy, World War II's most decorated soldier. The Texan returned with what we now call post-traumatic stress, suffering from insomnia, nightmares, and depression. Medication followed, and Murphy became addicted to the sleeping pill Placidyl. Aware of addiction's danger, Murphy locked himself in a motel room for a week, went through withdrawals, and came out clean.

Returning requires rediscovering meaning in something other than war. Medication, either legal or illegal, will not solve this problem. It is a temporary solution and, depending on the circumstances, it may be temporarily useful. But veterans cannot thrive in civilian life under any addictive influence, including prescription drugs. Fighting Exile means identifying what is and is not mental illness.

Exile hates this self-mastery. Its forces are discontented demons, seeking to prevent the warrior from applying combat knowledge toward some peaceful purpose. Exile compels the veteran to sit around and fantasize about the good old days in command or in the fight, choking out the future with illusions of the past. Exile traps you there forever—chewing apart your humanity with happy, haunted memories and smothering your soul into empty, stoned oblivion.

10

DEFEATING EXILE
TAKES TIME

Well-intentioned counselors often drive transitioning veterans to "have a plan" for how they will earn a civilian living. These plans could be everything from using veterans benefits to attend college to going back to work in a family business.

Long before Joseph Campbell, another great writer related Exile to the warrior's journey. Three thousand years ago, Homer wrote of Odysseus, Western civilization's original warrior in Exile. Odysseus had a plan for returning too—he had been fighting the Trojans for ten years. A wife, family, and

glorious riches awaited him back in Ithaca. It was a
solid transition strategy.

But no plan survives first contact with Exile.
Odysseus had included Aeolus in his return
approach, and the wind god had sealed all breezes
except the western wind in a leather bag. This
should have ensured a safe trip back to Ithaca, but
unfortunately his crew opened the bag looking for
plunder just as his hometown emerged in sight.
The winds of Exile burst forth and blew the ship
off course, beginning *The Odyssey*'s tale of trials
and temptations. For another decade, Odysseus
endured a torturous physical, mental, emotional
and psychological journey back home.

While aggressive transition approaches make
military recruiters a lot of money—who doesn't
want to hire dependable, hard-working heroes
who will get things done no matter what?—such
planning rarely honors the spiritual space a warrior
needs to shed old skin and evolve. As the Native
Americans knew, defeating Exile does not just take
comrades. It also takes time.

If you are a combat veteran in therapy, you probably
know you should mentally and emotionally process
the convoy when the MRAP in front of you exploded,
or the stench of decomposing insurgent carcasses

following a firefight, or the patrol when your squad leader's blood splattered you after a bullet shattered his brain. You want to talk, but it takes time to explain what you went through.

Conversely, it can be difficult to talk about what you didn't go through. What if you went to war but never killed? Are you a weaker person if you were hit but, lacking a target, held your fire? Does restraint count for as much valor as aggression? And how can you talk with people who weren't there, who didn't even volunteer to fight?

Finally, it takes time for a warrior to make his or her combat experience meaningful. What is your calling—your real one, not your job title or military occupational specialty? What offers you excitement, enthusiasm and purpose? And how does combat make you better at that?

These are hard questions, which is why returning veterans often benefit from not having any other plan besides returning. Everyone has a different timeline, but planning for a year of attacking Exile is a helpful starting point. For some it will be more; for others less. For a few, it may take a decade or more. Sadly, a small number may never return.

Psychologist Jonathan Shay, who worked with Vietnam veterans in Boston, describes Exile well in *Odysseus in America*, which uses the Trojan warrior's tribulations as metaphors for veterans struggling through post-traumatic stress. The pain of being among civilians, flights from boredom, urges to stay in combat mode, feelings that no place is safe, sinister memories, guilt, addictions and lies, coldness and cruelty to loved ones. It's all there. Nothing is new.

The Exile we now call PTSD has been there for all of humanity's traumatic history, from Odysseus' crippled crew to today's Wounded Warrior Regiments. Even if psychologists, veterans affairs administrators, and human resources counselors had existed back in Ithaca, they wouldn't have been enough to lead a warrior like Odysseus through Exile.

Depending on their complexity, animals and plants grow and evolve from stage to stage. Some changes are slow and invisible; others are sharp and immediate. But growing is never easy. If it was, it wouldn't be growth.

11

DEFEATING EXILE REQUIRES COMRADES

Whenever a small unit—team, squad, section, platoon, company—endures a major firefight or casualties, the warriors often sit together to talk about what happened, how they feel, and what to do next. This is a good thing: units celebrate their accomplishments when they gain victory and mourn the price paid in blood. Throughout the U.S. military, generals commonly tell junior leaders to conduct these conversations as part of combat training, sustainment and recovery.

The focus when deployed, however, is not on returning a warrior to civilian life. These discussions—as well as many of the military's official wounded warrior recovery programs— are about returning to battle. The same goes for conversations with psychologists, doctors and chaplains. No matter the counselor, commanders only have one question: when can the warrior fight? When will they be mentally and physically capable of rejoining the team?

Returning veterans need comrades too. Whether shipmates or strangers, soldiers or sisters, the friends you can count on can offer humor, understanding, and empathy. They can bolster you ahead in ways only you know you need. This was the second stage that Joseph Campbell's returning heroes went through: discovering the right guides who point the way back from the noble quest.

But part of discovering your community of comrades is figuring out where you're trying to go. What is the final stage in your return? What does it mean to defeat Exile—for you, not anyone else? What do you want your life to look like? Do you trust where these comrades are taking you?

If returning to battle takes time, then integrating the wisdom gained from combat—and trusting spouses, siblings, colleagues and friends who have never been there with your experiences and emotions— can be even more difficult. This is the final, and most challenging, of Campbell's stages: mastering the dualities of two opposite domains.

12

DEFEATING EXILE REQUIRES MASTERY

The hero's ultimate goal is thriving in two contradictory worlds. The capacity to move comfortably between conflicting philosophical systems comes from wisdom acquired through trials endured. By the story's end—in myth and life—material and spiritual conflicts coexist, reconciled in a balanced soul. They are in the world, but not of it. Both peace and war are affirmed.

What does mastery of two worlds mean? In *The Last Samurai*, Ken Watanabe's Lord Katsumoto appears as contented studying new languages or meditating in his quiet dojo as he does flinging his army into a flanking maneuver or lopping off his enemy's head. Andy Dufresne, unjustly convicted in *The Shawshank Redemption*, masters criminal deception and defeats an evil prison boss, illegally smuggling himself out of jail and stealing back his life. Katsumoto used peaceful meditation to focus his warrior awareness, calmed by the thought of "a good death." Dufresne was a clean man on the outside, but "had to go to prison to become a crook."

"The test of a first-rate intelligence is the ability to hold two opposed ideas in mind at the same time and still retain the ability to function," said F. Scott Fitzgerald. "One should, for example, be able to see things as hopeless and yet be determined to make them otherwise."

This is what returning requires. This is the end state the homecoming warrior seeks; the emotional and psychological place they are trying to find. Once you have mastered both worlds, you have defeated Exile. This is also why transitioning is so hard. Mastery doesn't happen overnight.

Accepting any two contradictions as equally meritorious will bring either genius or cognitive dissonance; spiritual tranquility or suicidal despair. Our goal, in both cases, is more of the former and less of the latter. Returning happens each day, as we master the yin and yang of opposite truths. This fills us with freedom, creates clarity and confidence, and brings awareness and meaning as we work to make our combat experiences integral to vibrant, extraordinary civilian lives.

13

DEFEATING EXILE
IS ON YOU

Like violence in combat, the path to defeating Exile runs on a spectrum. Either we are finding a place to reconcile both war and peace, or we are unhappy at home and confused in combat. But whatever the progression or regression, the outcome's ultimate resolution is our own. There is no psychologist, program or pill that can provide passion, power and peace.

Politicians on all sides are fond of proclaiming government's importance in veterans affairs. While it is appropriate for a government that sends youth into war to provide medical care, college tuition, and social benefits to enable transition, it is not the government's job to give grown men and women destinies, desires and dreams. Government leaders and civic activists can and should do many things for veterans, but the VA and Wounded Warrior Project cannot defeat Exile. Only you can.

Like each veteran's war, every Exile is different. Consequently, each veteran's mastery of war and peace will be expressed in different, individual ways. The beautiful and beastly brew of war's triumphal and toxic emotion can and does have a peaceful purpose if you are willing to find it.

Let me say that again: combat can make you a better civilian.

Do you believe that?

If not, stop reading.

If you do not think you can live a healthy and productive life in civilian society, put this book down and figure out a way to go back to war. Sign up with the French Foreign Legion. Get a job with G4S or another security contractor. Go to Uganda, South Sudan, or the Congo and join some warlord's resistance army. Just browse *Soldier of Fortune*; there are plenty of places to fight.

But if you want to return, you will have to evaluate for yourself how that happens for you spiritually as well as practically. Is there a place for martial virtues like courage in civilian society? Do any of combat's principles have a useful peacetime application? If so, what does that look and feel like? How do you actually go about mastering two opposite worlds?

Perhaps you feel guilt over enemies you killed or friends you could not save. Perhaps you're traumatized by the intensity of everything you endured. Even if therapy gives you coping skills for the guilt or trauma, it won't give you an identity. The fight against Exile is a normal challenge on the road to return—the VA cannot save you from it. Exile does not care about your disability rating—it goes after you no matter what.

Do you want to return? If so, you must affirm that to yourself. You must believe your combat experience makes you a better citizen. You're a veteran, not a victim. Eventually, you'll discover a new professional identity that your time in combat will enhance.

But before you do that, you'll have to work with the civilians around you to communicate the paradox of war and peace. Can you confront and accept both of these bipolar worlds? War is a difficult thing to explain to civilians, and peace can be hard for warriors to accept.

Are war and peace compatible? They can be. But only if you can honestly describe to yourself and your closest civilian comrades what war and peace are. As a veteran, you know war's charisma can also be criminal, and peacetime's simple pleasures can sometimes bring on puzzling pain.

Our next challenge is reconciling these contradictions.

PART TWO
DUALITY

14

WAR IS NOT LIKE ANYTHING ELSE

In the United States, we use "war" to mean a lot of things.

An exciting athletic contest becomes a war between two evenly matched competitors. This is thrilling, but it is not war.

Businesses go to war with each other over consumer products, management rights, and market share. Competitive, but not war.

Unhappily married couples fight legal battles over rights when dividing property and progeny to separate their previously united lives. Unpleasant, but also not war.

Movies, video games, and television shows create fictive violent constructs to entertain and satisfy audiences. These diversions sometimes trigger primal emotions. Clearly not war.

As mentioned, the human condition's more unpleasant manifestations—poverty, corpulence, joblessness, inequality, narcotics, and slow wi-fi connections—often pit expensive government programs against inanimate, enduring social ills. With a few notable exceptions—seat belts, drunk driving, littering along Texas highways—the human condition usually wins. Some of these programs are noble. Some are banal. But these efforts are not war.

Finally, many people term the daily struggle against their character flaws and internal demons as an "inner war" or a "spiritual war." Islamic scholars often say this is the true meaning of the Arabic word *jihad*. The Christian apostle Paul referred to this daily effort in martial terms, defining the choice of good over evil as "putting on the armor of God." This ongoing struggle to serve, as President Abraham Lincoln said, "the better angels of our nature" may lead to significant spiritual conversions and meaningful life events.

But, once again, it is not war.

15

METAPHOR WAR VS. REAL WAR

War is part of the human condition. It has been, is, and will be somewhere on the planet for the remainder of our lifetimes. Not metaphor war. Real War.

Real War, which is both an art and a science, is violent human competition. Real War cannot be separated from violence. Real War involves aggressive, threatening, dominating, physical assertion between two or more peoples competing to control each other in mind, body and spirit. This assertion of power and will, or its credible threat, has been part of human interaction since the dawn of time.

In the United States today, Real War is not typically part of human interaction—although there are exceptions. Street gangs may attack and defend pitches of asphalt, concrete, and brick turf. Travel and migration can bring awareness of combat. Grandparents, parents, relatives or friends may have fought and taught hidden, dangerous truths through their stories.

But now, if you're a combat veteran, you are part of the small minority of Americans who know:

Real War is nothing like metaphor war.

16

RETURNING FROM WAR IS NOT LIKE RETURNING FROM ANYTHING ELSE

The return from war to peace, from warrior to citizen, does not fully compare with any other experience. The closest contrast might be walking from a darkroom into brilliant sunlight. Going from Olympian athlete to regular Joe is intense, but it is still not the same as military to civilian.

"Boys with a normal viewpoint were taken out of the fields and offices and factories and classrooms and put into the ranks," explained Major General Smedley Butler, USMC, comparing the World War I veteran's transition to military drill. "They were remolded; they were made over; they were made to *about face*; to regard murder as the order of the day. They were put shoulder to shoulder and, through mass psychology, they were entirely changed.

"Then, suddenly, we discharged them and told them to make another *about face*. This time they had to do their own readjustment, without mass psychology, without officer aid and advice, and without nationwide propaganda. We didn't need them anymore. Many, too many, of these fine young boys are eventually destroyed, mentally, because they could not make that final *about face* alone."

Major General Butler was writing about the return of Americans who fought in World War I's gruesome trenches. These men went to war for a country that, in their absence, elected a temperate Congress that welcomed them back by prohibiting alcohol. Talk about a letdown.

The general was right in his description, but wrong in his prescription. On the contrary, the only way a veteran can return is by making that final *about face* alone.

Society can help—and it is morally obligated to do so. Comrades and guides can point out signposts and steps. But the return is like death: there's a million ways to do it. All you need is one.

To make that final *about face*, both veterans and civilians must understand the immense chasm between the values, ethics and origins of their respective environments. One you have seen both war and peace, it's impossible to view either in the same way.

17

DEFINITIONS AND DUALITIES

Although war and peace have evolved throughout history, their natures have remained constant. But for most Americans, who view peace as the normal state of human relations, peace is seen as good, while war is bad. This makes warriors social outcasts to some degree because they volunteered to dedicate their life to a violent calling. Aware of war's intensity, civilians borrow the language for, well, "civil" purposes, making war against social problems that don't involve killing. This is a problem for returning warriors, who have lived and thrived in an environment that is the opposite of peace.

Peace is war's antithesis. It is not necessarily better or worse than war. It is, however, the inverse of war in just about every respect. Strangely enough, the line separating war and peace has blurred in recent generations. Instead of combat operations, troops deploy on peacekeeping missions. This suggests they are in a place where peace can be kept, which of course may not be true at all. As we have seen in malls, college campuses, movie theaters, and elementary school classrooms, peace has been difficult to keep even in the most modern countries.

When we contrast the jungle with the desert, or a mountain lake with an urban neighborhood, we are not saying one is better than the other. On the contrary, we define each setting in relation to its opposite, and this gives us the tools we need to thrive in the new environment. Can an umbrella protect you from a sandstorm? Would you take a wool coat to the beach?

War and peace are different. In many ways they are polar opposites. At the same time, they both have the capacity to enhance or destroy the human spirit. For this reason, part of returning can involve examining the defining characteristics of both atmospheres, looking at each as a side of the same coin.

Describing war and peace enables warriors to comprehend these bipolar environments and master their contrasting dualities. And when civilians know how to talk about where warriors have been, they will better understand the psychological tools veterans require to return.

18

WAR IS CONFUSION

War, the English word, derives from several European languages. The Old English *wyrre*, Old North French *werre*, and Old High German *werran* (as well as their Spanish, Italian, and Portuguese form *guerra*) all originated from the German *verwirren*. This verb meant "to confuse or perplex."

War is confusion. War's science requires tactics and techniques; its art depends on instincts and intuitions. War is boredom punctuated by insanity—a hurricane of choices, emotions, and reactions centered on rapidly changing circumstances almost impossible to fully understand.

General James Mattis, the Marine Corps warrior monk, understood war as confusion. Hence his radio call sign: Chaos.

Because war requires disorder, it is incredibly difficult to describe with clarity to those who haven't been there. In part, confusion propagates exponentially because no warrior's experience is the same, even when sharing identical circumstances. This chaos impacts anyone who endures it for life.

Sometimes warriors can accept this paradox more easily than civilians. But regardless, the process of communicating this confusion is exceptionally overwhelming. No one returns from war without feeling confused. Can you swim in the ocean without getting wet?

The violent, mortal aggressions of war are among the most complex, chaotic and consequential human experiences any person can be subjected to on the planet. Is it any wonder that combat veterans struggle to describe their experience to a civilian who has never been there? Is it a surprise they are confused when asked to explain what they have endured?

19

PEACE IS ORDER

Have you ever been to Switzerland? There's an extraordinary sense of order that permeates this peaceful society. Watches, knives, and bank accounts are dependable and function in flawless synergy. The country's major cities, Geneva and Zurich, are annually ranked as the world's best places to live. Protected by the Alps, the Swiss managed to achieve neutrality during both of Europe's twentieth century catastrophes. Was this a moral accomplishment or luck from defensive terrain? Or both?

During the mid-twelfth century, the Anglo-French word *pes* grew to mean "freedom from civil disorder," an expression encompassing not only the absence of war but also the assurance of social harmony. A free people have overcome the scourge of war and obtained calm. They are not threatened by exterior or interior violence. They fear neither invasions nor school shootings. They have order.

The Swiss have an interesting social relationship with war and peace. Switzerland does not maintain a standing army, but almost every Swiss man between twenty and thirty serves at some point in the militia. Fewer than five percent of Swiss Army veterans are professional soldiers; the rest are conscripts who keep their weapons and equipment at home. The eight million Swiss citizens have the highest gun ownership rate in the world. And yet, with only forty homicides involving firearms in 2010, the Swiss also have one of the lowest ratios of firearm ownership to violent death.

Switzerland appears to have evolved into an orderly, peaceful society not by eliminating violence or pretending it does not exist. On the contrary, Switzerland's order seems to flow from social bonds formed by training together for the most chaotic event humans can ever experience, and then hoping it never happens.

20

WAR IS EXERTION

The modern German word for war, *krieg*, derives from Middle High German *kriec* which meant "exertion, enmity, opposition." Americans know this word best from the Nazi word *blitzkrieg*, or flash war (literally, war in a lightning instant). But *krieg* as a root word is less about speed than exertion, and was more associated in previous generations with its close cousin *kampf*, or struggle.

Every day, seven billion people wake up and struggle to satisfy nature's exacting requirements: food, water and shelter. Next, they look to gain love or power by exchanging commodities. Some are privileged enough to then seek meaning and purpose behind this exertion.

But how many of these seven billion exert themselves beyond a struggle against nature? How many fight for dominance against rivals who literally, not metaphorically, seek to kill them?

The warrior does. Warriors confront exertion against an opposing force whose hatred is fierce enough to take their lives. Warriors respond to this opposition with physical, mental, and emotional energy—channeling hostility and anger against the opponent desiring their death.

The enemy chases the warrior. Sweat pours. Lungs and ligaments scream for more oxygen. Concealed, the warrior seeks their enemy. The rifle settles into the shoulder; the trigger pulls; the bolt slides forward; the bullet impacts. The warrior lives. His enemy dies.

Not today, you sons of whores, thinks the warrior, bubbling with passionate exertion against his enemy's deadly quest. *You will not kill me today*.

21

PEACE IS AMBIVALENT

When it was commonly used, the Latin nominative *pax*, like the Spanish *paz* and Italian *pace*, had multiple meanings. The *Pax Romana* was not only Rome's prevention of war; it also pointed toward the indifference of any other power rising to challenge Roman authority. In this way, peace is ambivalent—indifferent to fighting for protection or exercising aggression.

If war demands exertion to achieve an outcome, peace is apathetic toward the forces shifting around it. Most of nature is not at peace; salmon swimming upstream are in near-constant labor, as are moose rutting for status during mating season. Most species are not indifferent about their survival.

In contrast, peace goes with the flow around controlling forces, coexisting within whatever constraints the elements and environment allow. Peace is a shimmering lake at dawn, undisturbed by any element. Peace wields force against nothing and enacts controls on no one.

I once asked a family member who claimed to be a pacifist how she would respond if physically attacked. Would she fight back? No, she said. She would curl up into a ball and wait until either someone else fought off her attacker or she died. Like many Americans, she is not a violent person. Unlike many Americans, she is fully prepared to accept the consequences of her nonviolence.

While I appreciated her honesty and self-awareness, I would not be comfortable with ambivalence in such a circumstance. Likewise, most citizens are not uncertain about this dichotomy. Most of us are just like the salmon and moose and every other species. In our fight for survival, we are highly unlikely to accept peace at any price.

22

WAR IS BEAUTIFUL

In the middle ages, Anglo-Saxon tribes may have turned to the Germanic language to define war because they wanted to avoid the Latin *bellum*, which the Romans commonly used. It comes from *bello* and means "beautiful."

War is beautiful, and not only for the sentimental comradeship and bonding. Because warriors deal in imminent death, they operate in a zone free from daily distractions. The heightened awareness makes death just another part of life, giving each moment meaning. Warriors don't have to read new age advice books telling them how important it is to "live in the moment." They can't exist in any other place. All they have is that instant, that action, that single breath.

Beyond the spiritual beauty, winning, or even just surviving, a bellicose firefight produces stratospheric adrenaline levels. For Americans in Iraq and Afghanistan, this sensation extended to convoys or patrols that went "outside the wire," which entailed greater danger than staying on a secure base. Neurologists and psychologists have compared this euphoria with a drug. This is why the thrill of a firefight can be as addictive as narcotics.

Camaraderie, clarity, and charm: war has a charisma all its own. Warriors struggle to move beyond its glory when society does not allow them to acknowledge its true beauty. "It is well that war is so terrible," said Confederate General Robert E. Lee, watching his army repulse a Union charge during the 1862 Battle of Fredericksburg, "otherwise we should grow too fond of it."

"I love it," said General George S. Patton, misty-eyed, inhaling battlefield smoke as depicted in the 1970 film. "God help me, I do love it so."

23

PEACE IS QUIET

The modern French *paix* first emerged as peace in the eleventh century. Its synonym was the French *silence*, which means the same thing in English. Peace is soundless stillness and untroubled tranquility. Peace is quiet.

In human terms, we define peace by conjuring mental images of people in silent repose. A monk meditates. A baby sleeps. A writer ruminates with her coffee cup. An athlete breathes in his sun salute. A performer closes her eyes and visualizes. All are at peace.

"Men lead lives of noisy desperation," said James Thurber. By connecting peace with quiet, we acknowledge something unspoken about what it takes for us simple humans to reconcile ourselves with, well...with ourselves. Conflict exists inside each human spirit, and resolving this inner tension requires some measure of seclusion.

There's a reason we refer to distractions in our lives as noise—the thoughts keeping us from peace. "True silence is the rest of the mind," said William Penn. "It is to the spirit what sleep is to the body." Quiet enables leaders to be at peace in their decisions.

"Solitude is the very essence of leadership," said William Deresiewicz to the West Point Class of 2013 during their plebe year. "The position of the leader is ultimately an intensely solitary, even intensely lonely one." Lincoln and Gandhi would agree, as would Confucius, whose maxims also bring mental pictures of quiet peace. "Silence is the true friend that never betrays," he said.

And quiet is not only evidence of peace; it is also a key to maintaining it. "He that would live in peace and at ease," said Benjamin Franklin, "must not speak all he knows or all he sees."

24

WAR IS CRUELTY

Although war does mean confusion, beauty, and exertion, these words and accompanying ideas do not fully capture the brutality of its venal character. "You cannot qualify war in harsher terms than I will," said Union General William Tecumseh Sherman. "War is cruelty, and you cannot refine it."

In the United States, distance and disconnect often obscure war's cruelty. Drone controllers launch weapons from remote aircraft, plunging steel into skin and ripping children's arms from torsos. This destruction eventually gets reduced to antiseptic, sterile language. Humans become high value targets. Bombings and attacks become kinetic operations or neutralization missions. Armed occupation becomes peacekeeping. The drone pilots drive home, hug their children, and try not to think about what they saw that day on their monitor screen.

Since death and pain are common in war, inflicting pain on one's opponent is to some degree an environmental necessity. Torturing captured insurgents or urinating on their corpses may be inhumane, but so is detonating bombs in a wedding reception or launching mortars into a street market.

This is why enduring cruelty without literally taking an eye for an eye poses such immense psychological pressure. As General Sherman understood, cruelty can prevent the enemy from embarking on a path of equally cruel destruction. Theorists, politicians, and academics talk about "the credible use of force." Force is not kind persuasion. Force is fierce coercion.

A veteran returns. Thrilled to be alive; euphoric over personal victories; entranced with the battlefield's beauty. But also haunted by ambitions; confused by war's romance; and deeply aware that war, despite its paradoxical virtue, is the ultimate expression of our collective inhumanity.

25

PEACE IS SAFETY

From Christianity's earliest days, one of the key moments in the communion ceremony was the "sign of peace" fellowship members would offer one another. In secular terms, the handshake was the greeting that took form in Greece and Rome as a peace sign, serving to demonstrate that no weapon was hidden under sleeves. The Hebrew word for peace, *shalom*, expresses the same feeling.

These greetings exist to communicate both spiritual and physical safety. Like a baby sleeping innocently in a stroller, to be at peace is to be in a safe, protected place. Absent war, absent hostility, absent confusion. Free from risk or danger or fear.

The great irony of life, however, is that no person grows, develops, or matures without challenging themselves and taking risks that inherently create fear and force them beyond their comfort zone. Spiritually, financially, physically, professionally: achievement and evolution demand movement beyond a safe place.

Peace is safety. But eternal peace—at least in this world—will always be an illusion. Whether in external life circumstances or one's own soul, it is conflict, not peace, which precipitates true growth.

26

WAR IS NOBLE

"War is an ugly thing," wrote the British philosopher John Stuart Mill, "but not the ugliest of things. The decayed and degraded state of moral and patriotic feeling which thinks that nothing is *worth* a war is much worse."

This quote comes from *The Contest in America*, an essay published in the February 1862 issue of *Harper's Magazine*. A year into the American Civil War, many English politicians were calling for Lincoln's government to end the war and grant the Confederacy freedom. Mill saw the war as a noble struggle to end slavery, and he wrote in philosophical defense of the Union's honor.

"When a people are used as mere human instruments for firing cannon or thrusting bayonets, in the service and for the selfish purposes of a master, such war degrades a people," continued Mill, distinguishing between an unjust and just war. "A war to protect other human beings against tyrannical injustice...is often the means of their regeneration."

And who does Mill pity? "A man who has nothing which he is willing to fight for," said Mill, "nothing which he cares more about than he does about his personal safety, is a miserable creature who has no chance of being free unless made and kept so by the exertions of better men than himself."

In the United States, we rightfully honor those who volunteer for military service because their actions demonstrate the answer to this question: they would die for you. "Greater love hath no man than this: that a man lay down his life for his friends," the Scriptures say. Like the samurai's unflinching code of honor, a noble war offers meaning and purpose.

For whom are you willing to die? For what would you sacrifice your life? War demands and offers answers to these questions. But beyond law enforcement, medical rescue, and firefighting, is there any civilian calling that can fully match this force of meaning and nobility the warrior discovers?

27

PEACE IS FREEDOM

Peace is also derived from Latin *pagus*, from which we obtain the French *pays* and Spanish *pais*. These words mean country, region, land. A place of peace, where life and liberty are not under threat. A place of freedom, occupied by people immune from the fear of imminent death.

Any country, region, or land stricken by war's scourge is under the tyranny of its unpredictable and chaotic fortunes. By definition, this type of *pagus* is not at liberty. Such a place is not a *pais*, but merely soil under siege. Only the peaceful place is free.

Combat, in contrast, constricts a warrior's individual identity. War may be beautiful, but those who pledge their lives, fortunes, and sacred honor to its conduct are not living as free citizens. From the Athenian Army to Al Qaeda; from Montezuma's Aztecs to the Marine Corps, martial conduct demands a hierarchy. War may lead to liberty, but it cannot exist alongside it.

Those who have volunteered for war know this. They are acutely aware that they have given up certain freedoms while wearing the uniform. In part, they may have chosen to do so believing they could only experience a feeling of freedom if they paid a debt to society. In return, when they returned, society would compensate them, both in fiscal and communal reward, for their service.

"Peace is liberty in tranquility," said Cicero, describing what *pax* meant to Roman citizens—and to the regions that remained free from chaos and strife. Cicero never served in the military, but he eventually became one of Rome's leading citizens— dying only after Marc Antony made war upon him after Julius Caesar's assassination. Some scholars believe Cicero's lack of military service was one of Antony's grievances against him. Antony didn't think Cicero had earned the right to lead Rome.

If this was Antony's attitude, he was wrong. In the military-civilian social contract, both parties owe something to the other. Society owes veterans gratitude for their willingness to sacrifice. But veterans also owe citizens the recognition and affirmation that peace, not war, defines true freedom.

28

WAR IS CRIMINAL

War is beautiful, valiant, and noble. But it is not innocent. Most of the core competencies professional combat requires—assault, surprise, deception—are criminal actions in the civilian world. The Spartans took this to an extreme, teaching their novice fighters to steal for survival as part of their curriculum in the *agoge*. The youth were punished only if caught, as successful thievery was understood as a requirement for victory on the battlefield.

"All war is deception," said Chinese philosopher Sun Tzu. Enlisted soldiers lie to their superiors, believing the battlefield atrocity they commit is ethical if it makes the enemy fear them. Officers mislead generals, claiming responsibility for successes they haven't achieved in the hopes they will be promoted and granted more authority. Generals deceive politicians, asking for more money, more troops, more resources, so they can remain in the field and sate their glorious ambitions.

"War is a racket," wrote Major General Smedley Butler in 1938, offering remarkable candor while reflecting on his career. "It is possibly the oldest, easily the most profitable, surely the most vicious. It is the only one international in scope. It is the only one in which the profits are reckoned in dollars and the losses in lives." Deception is not war's only criminality. From Pierre du Pont to Erik Prince, war has been an exercise in civilian profiteering as much as conquest.

"This bill renders a horrible accounting," continues Butler, whose words call to mind a balance sheet and ledger that anyone favoring unlimited war should calculate. "Newly placed gravestones. Mangled bodies. Shattered minds. Broken hearts and homes. Economic instability. Depression and all its attendant miseries. Back-breaking taxation for generations and generations."

A criminal racket indeed.

29
PEACE IS AGREEMENT

The Latin word for peace, *pax*, originally stood for the absence of war, particularly when guaranteed by an empirical overlord (as in *Pax Romana*). From this we get the noun *pact*, our English word for a covenant or agreement.

Where war is deception and strife, peace is truth and tranquility. Peace is seeing eye to eye. Peace is a handshake. Peace is concurrence, alignment, synergy, resolution. Peace is conflict's antithesis. Once agreement is reached, conflict ends.

Pacts, like peace, can come and go. They shift depending on human emotion. Each individual soul has its own ambition. Different ambitions lead to different interests, and those lead to conflict. Resolving those ambitions and interests brings peace.

Many warriors—particularly men serving in infantry units—achieve peace in combat within their small circle. When each member of a team, squad, detachment, or platoon sees things eye to eye with the other, they are at war, but at peace within war. Warriors have a name for this enigmatic harmony: unit cohesion. Inside the unit, people agree.

Even at war people look for peace. And even in peace people still feel some level of conflict, whether agreements remain temporary or endure for generations.

30

WAR IS POLITICAL

If politics is the great human drama, war is the climax of almost every act. "War is not merely an act of policy," said Prussian general Carl von Clausewitz, "but a true political instrument—a continuation of political intercourse carried on through other means."

The word politics comes from Greek *politikos*, meaning "relating to citizens." War (or the threat thereof) is inseparable from a state, city, or person's exercise of political power on behalf of its own citizenry. The ability to make war, to use violence or intimidation to achieve action, is directly tied to the political authority one seeks to gain or retain.

Although New York, Washington D.C., and, most recently, Boston, are notable exceptions, war exists in a realm far removed from American citizens. While this is good, few things make combat veterans more cynical than casual political conversation trivializing their actions. Half the citizenry says they should "kill them over there instead of over here." The other half says we should come home so all the killing can stop. Nobody wants to talk about it or to hear what the war was really like.

And oddly enough, nobody seems to care that combat veterans might feel emotional over places they fought for being lost to enemy flags. It's impossible for Iraq or Afghanistan veterans not to take the rise of the Islamic State in Iraq and Syria or the Taliban's threat to Afghanistan's future personally. Sometimes American citizens seem to value ending war more than they do winning it.

But in the end, the war is for them. The citizens. It is of them, and civilians cannot wash their hands of it regardless of how many times they change the channel. Civilians who cannot own their political responsibilities as democratic voters leave returning veterans frustrated, confused, and unhinged. War dominates politics because violence is the ultimate arbiter of political authority once material coercion and moral persuasion have lost sway.

31

PEACE IS SPIRITUAL

Although we refer to war's conclusion as "reaching peace," this may do peace a disservice. This is because peace, unlike war, is not the great climax in a political human drama. Peace is something much more profound: the small internal climax in the great drama of each person's soul.

In this way, peace and war reveal truth in different realms. Politics involves the temporal pursuit or avoidance of war. Spirituality involves the ethereal quest to find truth inside oneself and then reveal that truth through one's daily living, which is the pursuit of inner peace.

In recent years, "peace studies" has become a popular undergraduate major on college campuses. This is a misnomer. To study peace suggests it can be achieved politically. It cannot, for politics inherently requires conflict.

Peace, on the contrary, is a spiritual quest. The spiritual realm, not the political one, is where the returning warrior must go when looking to find the way out of Exile. All the words we have associated with peace—order, agreement, ambivalence, freedom, safety—point toward an individual soul, not the body politic.

While making war requires a body politic (and a tax base), a human spirit at peace can be found almost anywhere in the world. Since warriors may discover profound peace inside themselves while enduring chaos, finding peace becomes one of the great complexities for warriors as they return home. If one can find inner peace at war—amidst confusion, chaos, and insanity—then how does a warrior do so in a normal civilian life?

"Whoever values peace of mind and the health of the soul will live the best of all possible lives," said the great Roman emperor Marcus Aurelius. He wrote these words while at war, leading the Roman Army from 166-180 C.E. in Germania.

32

WAR IS MASCULINE

Let me be clear: I mean no disrespect, offense or discrimination to the many women who are combat veterans with this statement. Women can shoot just as well, or better, than men. Courage under fire is not a male-only virtue. And women are quite capable of inspirational leadership through decisiveness, action and clarity while in command.

But in historical, legal, and psychological contexts, war is not a gender neutral sport. Its virtues and vices have defined and been ascribed to men for millennia. Society calls men to make war and asks men to defend themselves against other men who would inflict attack. Men either volunteer to fight for their society or pay other men to inflict violence (or threaten to do so) on their behalf.

Since 1917, when the United States entered World War I, the U.S. has maintained the Selective Service System, a conscription database that continues to this day. All male U.S. citizens (and most male U.S. legal residents) between the age of eighteen and twenty-five must register within thirty days of their eighteenth birthday. As of 2010, there are over 16.2 million men's names on file. Just in case.

Through the ages, the human psyche has evolved to seek rites of passage into adulthood through some type of heroic journey. For men, going on the warpath has often been one of these formal ceremonies or informal passage rites. But American society treats war as an interesting, gender neutral life experience. Consequently, civilians of both genders hesitate to publicly sanction combat service as a validation of masculinity.

By law, if freedom in our society is ever threatened, it will be fathers, brothers, husbands and sons whom the people hold responsible. Women can choose valor, and many do so with courage and honor. But for men, if society requires, the law demands their bravery. Like it or not, eons of social evolution have conditioned men to defend, protect and fight.

33

PEACE IS FEMININE

"If mothers ruled the world, there wouldn't be any goddamned wars," said actress Sally Field to loud applause at the 2007 Emmy Awards. Sally Field may have forgotten about Hillary Clinton. India's Indira Gandhi, Israel's Golda Meir, and the United Kingdom's Margaret Thatcher were all mothers who started wars.

But let's examine Field's assertion. Consider Greg Mortenson, who founded the Central Asia Institute to promote girls' education in Pakistan and Afghanistan, believing—not without cause—that women in social leadership roles were less likely to resolve conflict through violence. The view was widely held enough that Mortenson's book *Three*

Cups of Tea was mandatory reading for Americans deploying to Afghanistan, until writer Jon Krakauer exposed Mortenson as a fraud.

"I can promise you that women working together—linked, informed and educated—can bring peace and prosperity to this forsaken planet," said novelist Isabel Allende. The dominant American antiwar activist group is called Code Pink—another nod to the link between femininity and peace.

Women evolved to give birth and nurture the species. Right or wrong, men evolved to protect women as they did so. From a strictly primal perspective, any man in any society who cannot physically provide security is not fit to join the tribe.

How does this relate to a veteran's transition? As previously noted, the veteran community is overwhelmingly male. Many of those men subconsciously seek social validation for their willingness to fight and protect women. Again, there are exceptions, but for most warriors the tension between masculine and feminine endures. Just as war and peace are opposites, so also are their gender energies. In philosophic terms, peace represents female yin, while war is male yang.

To seek peace is to seek a cocoon of protection. A womb of safety. A feminine place.

34

WAR IS STOIC

"Man is disturbed not by things, but by the views he takes of them," wrote Epictetus. "That which Fortune has not given, she cannot take away," said Seneca. "The happiness of your life depends on the quality of your thoughts," meditated Marcus Aurelius.

Stoicism—willing submission to Fate; purging of futile desire; dispassionate striving for virtue— comprises the warrior's philosophical code. Vice Admiral James Stockdale, the senior U.S. Navy officer held prisoner in Hanoi in the Vietnam War, credited stoic thought with enabling him to perform honorably during his seven and a half years in captivity. Within the warrior culture, this focused transformation of passion into sacrificial action is called the "warrior mindset." Its doctrine is not found in Army manuals, but in stoic texts.

Because war is tribal, the warrior culture requires a philosophy that demands conformity to group ideals throughout combat's terror while also permitting the free thought necessary to cultivate virtue. Stoicism enables this. The stoic samurai who practice the profession embrace warrior values: valor, simplicity, austerity, sacrifice, frugality, endurance, and restraint.

Like all military cultures worldwide, Sparta—a modern synonym for war—might best be described as a socialist meritocracy. Placing emphasis on equality, honor, and virtue, these cultures have triumphed as mythical models of political development. From *300*'s fierce fortitude to Tough Mudder's camaraderie creed, civilians celebrate the simplicity of the warrior's spartan faith.

"I love the people of Boston," wrote Sam Adams in December 1780, suffering an extreme case of Laconophilia during the Revolution. "I once thought that city would be the Christian Sparta."

The returning veteran doesn't have to imagine Spartan stoicism through fantasy or games. Fortune has given them war. It is a gift, as Seneca might have said, that can never be taken away.

35

PEACE IS EPICUREAN

If stoic endurance defines war, then what is its opposite? For that, we look to Epicurus, the Athenian philosopher who argued that mankind finds meaning by seeking pleasure and avoiding pain. Epicurus, who served two years in the peacetime Athenian army before developing his philosophical doctrine, taught his followers to pursue simple joys, avoid politics, eschew organized religion, and seek self-sufficiency. Peace, as Thomas Jefferson wrote, is the pursuit of happiness.

While Americans may respectfully nod toward stoicism, our civilian lives are deeply rooted in Epicurean values. The polished, elegant furniture gleams off the living room's mirrors and skylights.

Lavender and mint waft through an aromatic hallway. The chef tastes garlic, onion, and oregano in his gravy as a chocolate soufflé bakes in the oven. Sinatra's romantic melodies and Mozart's gentle strains please ears and soothe spirits.

In the United States, civilians esteem such domestic delights. Jefferson, a self-proclaimed Epicurean, believed happiness was life's greatest goal. He chose his words carefully when declaring independence, striving in part to subordinate stoicism to epicurean philosophy. Taken another way, this duality frames the moral structure behind civilian control of military forces in the U.S. government.

This dichotomy also frames the challenge veterans have returning home. Transferring a skill is one thing—an Air Force helicopter mechanic can always look for work at Boeing or Bell Textron. Transferring values, ethos, and culture is another. Epicurean indulgences—delicious food, beautiful architecture, vibrant music—represent the antithesis of stoic warrior values.

The warrior's stoic socialist meritocracy is, for Americans, a system and structure pledged to defend its philosophical and cultural opposite: epicurean capitalism. Can both cultures be esteemed and respected by one another? Can stoic and epicurean values coexist?

36

WAR AND PEACE BOTH HAVE MEANING

War and peace both offer deep meaning. War and peace both bring life and death. War and peace can, potentially, both produce despair. War and peace are two sides of the human condition's coin. War and peace, in their many forms, make us what we are.

"It is an unfortunate fact that we can secure peace only by preparing for war," said President John F. Kennedy. "If we desire to secure peace," wrote General George Washington, "it must be known that we are at all times ready for war." Aristotle offers blunt summary: "We make war that we may live in peace."

The exertion, confusion, beauty and nobility of war bring a powerful and incomparable sense of purpose to a warrior community. The freedom, tranquility, safety, and simplicity of peace bring a profound and impenetrable happiness to human souls. To everything, there is a season.

Returning veterans must acknowledge this truth. The thought that peace could be as meaningful as war—that simple epicurean delights could bring as much satisfaction as hunting and destroying terrorists—is a huge bridge to cross. It is by far the most important. Otherwise, he may despise his civilian friends, or she is that much more likely to lash out in anger against caregiving or assistance. If peace brings scant meaning, then veterans will only want to return to war—to be back in the only place where they felt deep purpose. They will stay in Exile.

This is equally important for civilians. Whether or not a civilian supported the decision to go to war does not matter. The veteran fought because his stoic sense of duty demanded he earn status in his community. Because honor required her to offer herself as a willing and loving sacrifice for friends and family. Because courage commanded him to endure confusion, accept sorrow, bear burden and suffer tragedy. At some level, all veterans sought the wisdom and self-awareness from conflict and physical violence that makes war, or its credible risk, unlike any other human experience.

The answer to our earlier question is yes: the stoic and epicurean can coexist. The value of each opposite brings counterbalance to their inadequacies. "The object in war is a better state of peace," said military historian B.H. Liddell Hart, reminding the warriors of their ultimate purpose. "Peace is not an absence of war. It is a virtue, a state of mind, a disposition for benevolence, confidence, justice," said philosopher Baruch Spinoza, reminding the civilian that happiness can exist in war's hell.

So if we can accept that war and peace, even though they are opposites, can both have meaning, then what is our metric of success for returning veterans? As a society, how do we know if we are spending enough money on veterans' benefits if the state of peace they are seeking is ultimately a spiritual search? How can we, in President Lincoln's words, "care for him who shall have borne the battle" when the real conflict is in reconciling these dueling contradictions of the soul?

In American society, and in personal conversations, we must reconstruct the language of healing that has evolved in the United States over the past decade.

To find peace, warriors must be able to see their combat experience—no matter how traumatic—as something that can be as inspirational at home as it was necessary in war. As returning veterans, we must strive to appreciate post-traumatic stress as an invaluable asset for our growth rather than a permanent disorder that dooms us. Our physical and psychological scars must not become our downfall, but the fuel that makes us fly.

PART THREE

MASTERY

37

POST-TRAUMATIC STRESS ASSET

Before we go further, it's confession time. I don't have a formula or the answers to making it happen easily. I lack a simple fix to take you from Exile's despair to mastering two worlds. Although psychologists are researching post-traumatic growth, I can only offer my own experience.

I am not, have never been, and will never be a professional psychologist. I have not graduated from medical school or published a peer-reviewed depression article. Consequently, health insurance administrators or drug company lawyers may challenge my conclusions on why I think most veterans shouldn't waste money on diagnoses and drugs. But I think I make a reasonable argument. Why?

Because I believe veterans are not victims.

It's that simple. A veteran has gained knowledge from a different life experience. Those insights may be unconventional. They may challenge the status quo. They may offer a dynamic alternative or reveal a painful truth. But the place from which such wisdom comes can benefit us all.

As a combat veteran, you have resiliency. You have capacity. You can perform. You dream of something important—something you couldn't have accomplished without the perspective you gained from your warrior life. And now, because you can live as the master of two worlds...because you can appreciate both war and peace...because you can flow effortlessly from comfort to conflict...your vision can become real. Yes, you can grow from your trauma.

Warriors measure each other using courage as a metric. So what does courage look like as a civilian? Is it, perhaps, the simple audacity of self-awareness? Can you be true to who you really are and what you really want, no matter the cost? Can you obey your soul's authentic calling, even when friends and family think you're crazy? Do you have the guts to be true to yourself?

Damn right you do. That is Post-Traumatic Stress Asset.

38

THE CONTINUOUS FIGHT

My idea of PTSA does not end with an agenda or action plan. Instead, I offer observations for use as waypoints along your heroic journey home. These are the things I tell myself; I use them daily to return from Exile. They have helped me master the duality of two worlds. I hope they help you too.

Once, I was a professional warrior. Now, as a civilian, I research, travel and write. I also teach people how to explore with confidence, staying humble and self-aware in normal life and dangerous situations. I often go to unsafe places where others feel uncomfortable traveling, and my work offers creative and challenging ways to learn new things and serve my community. I enjoy the entrepreneurial nature of my career and have found it meaningful in my post-combat life.

When I left active duty, I wanted to make a courageous professional choice—to apply this central military virtue in a civilian context. For me, that meant having the guts to bet on myself as a writer, researcher, and advisor. I know other veterans who demonstrate courage while pursuing careers in finance, comedy, real estate, theater, energy, academia, home inspection, technology, farming, entertainment, politics, and science with little more than their own ambition. They offer portfolios, windmills, business proposals, *hors d'oeuvres*, self-defense classes, or poverty reduction programs in ways no one had thought of before. They have found meaning, purpose, and happiness while doing so.

They are my heroes. They defeat Exile. My hat's off to them.

Truth is, I am still trying to defeat Exile. Every day, I feel called more toward one world over the other. Sometimes I find the battlefield's energy comforting—a familiar camaraderie and brotherhood of combat's cruel secrets. Sometimes I never want to leave the four walls of my writing office—feeling safe in the cocoon of quiet professional rhythm. Sometimes I feel like that guy in *The Hurt Locker*. Sometimes I am not sure how to find balance.

39

TWO PATHS OF TRANSITIONS

According to Batya Rotter, an Israeli psychologist who researches military to civilian transitions, there are two different paths veterans take to defeat Exile. These two transition paths Rotter describes are not things veterans can choose for themselves; they are functions of the society from which they emerge. This context is important. As we have seen, American veterans come from and return to a society that does not easily comprehend their military identities.

Since Israel, like Switzerland, mandates military service, the development of a "soldier identity," as Rotter puts it, is a natural rite of passage. Israel is small enough that when the country goes to war, everyone is involved at some level. When veterans come back, they just don't talk about it. "Whatever issues they have, they block out and move on," Rotter said. They don't feel foreign or have any need to explain themselves. They did what they had to do and are eager to be civilians again.

Unlike after World War II, when returning GIs had a similar transition, few Americans today have direct military experience. Consequently, returning American veterans are often asked to discuss war in uncomfortable and confusing ways. Somebody once called me a hero because I was awarded a Purple Heart, a medal given to anyone wounded in combat. To me, that's like saying Muhammad Ali was courageous because he was punched in the face. There was nothing particularly gallant about my encounter with mortar shrapnel. It was a routine occupational hazard.

Since most U.S. civilians don't have a military identity, returning American veterans have the second transition path. Unlike countries with common military experience, American warriors must become relaxed in civil life while also staying true to the warrior roots that other citizens may not appreciate or accept. And civilians must grant the returning warriors understanding and affirmation of their ongoing military identities. Healthy transitions happen when veterans are comfortable toggling between their military and civilian identities and tapping into each in the appropriate context.

40

BE ORIGINAL

The warrior culture offers a bountiful community environment. My own tribe, the Marine Corps, takes pride in being a year older than the United States. Marine traditions span multiple generations—some are bawdy, some are extraordinary, some are powerful, some are even true. These traditions create profound meaning. Once you are a part of them, your life is never quite the same.

But do I miss the Marines? While I have great memories and fond friendships from my time in service, there is one thing I have as a civilian that the Marine Corps could never provide.

I can be my own individual.

Remember our discussion of stoic/political versus epicurean/spiritual? Warrior cultures are built to develop conformist virtues: self-sacrifice, commitment, endurance. These values represent the community ties that bind warriors to society.

But in the United States, where each life is granted liberty to pursue happiness, the freedom of discovering and profiting from a true, original passion—electricity, assembly line automobiles, light bulbs, storytelling, airplanes, hydraulic fracking, iPads—is what makes civilian life great.

Originality has limited value in military life. Even though Marines no longer carry swords, shields, and spears, they still pray to the Spartan and Samurai gods of tribe and community devotion before battle. In contrast, every American has the right—indeed, a certain duty—to invent an independent identity. Individual expression is not just part of civilian life—it *is* civilian life.

"Don't ever think you cannot do something just because you haven't done it before," says entrepreneur coach Matt Furey. "It's perfectly natural to go after things in life that are totally new."

Want to master two worlds? Use courage gained in combat to do something original.

41

THE FLAVOR OF FREEDOM

In 1966, Tim Craft graduated high school in Kansas. His main interests, besides girls, were marching band and debate, and he wanted to become a lawyer. Vaguely aware of the Vietnam War, Craft enrolled in junior college, paying his way by working nights at a clothing company.

When he joined the Marine Corps, Craft's professors and employers begged him to reconsider. Craft said he didn't feel right getting ahead in life while other young men his age were forced to do something he wasn't. By February 1968, Lance Corporal Tim Craft, now an ammunition technician, was halfway into a combat tour, under siege with six thousand

Marines at Khe Sanh Air Base. For seventy-seven days, an average of one thousand mortar, artillery, and rocket shells pummeled the base daily.

During the siege, Craft spotted a reporter, called him over, said something and asked him to get the message back to the world. The journalist looked surprised and asked the Marine to write it down. Craft did so, scrawling what later became an inspiration to Vietnam veterans on a C-ration case. "For those that will fight for it," Craft wrote, "freedom has a flavor the protected shall never know."

To the warrior, freedom is sweeter than the purest honey, syrup, or cane sugar ever produced. When Lance Corporal Craft wrote his message, he was not justifying war. He was trying to capture his depth of emotion, the way a man dying of thirst explains water.

The returning warrior must find a way to celebrate the joy of freedom. Embracing this elation among comrades, both former and current, both warrior and civilian, makes the simple pleasures of peace that much more powerful.

Warriors can celebrate individual liberty by pursuing an original life and calling of their choice. Discovering meaning and purpose in civilian life gives their earned independence authenticity, energy and texture.

What is the flavor of freedom? Whatever amazing concoction you create.

42

LIFE IS SHORT

In 2005, I boarded a plane at Chicago O'Hare Airport. I had just driven round trip from Milwaukee, having completed an emotional series of interviews with Brian Zmudzinski. An Iraq war veteran, Zmudzinski's squad leader and dear friend, Daniel Amaya, had died alongside him. I took my seat absentmindedly, the cabin door closed, and I drifted into a reverie. Twenty minutes passed and we still hadn't moved. The captain made one announcement, then another. The inspection revealed a damaged part, he said. Then he suggested they might need a crew change while the part was installed.

As our ground waiting time approached an hour, the man sitting to my left fumed and cursed. He needed a reroute; his schedule was destroyed; something awful (or so he thought) would befall him if immediate action didn't happen. Unless I found a way off the plane, I was stuck with this guy. Finally, I cut him off in mid-rant. "You know," I said, "things could be worse."

It is not always appropriate for veterans to remind civilians they've been to war. Sometimes it can be obnoxious, arrogant, or rude. But in this case, I was calm. For me, that's usually a good indicator to decide whether I should discuss my military identity.

I told my fulminating friend I thought it was a pretty good day when I wasn't getting mortared and shot at. Besides the risk of our plane crashing, nothing bad would happen to us. We would get where we wanted to go. Everything would work out. I didn't tell him about Amaya, but he got the idea. We talked on and off for another two hours. I don't remember his name.

What I remember was that I gave him perspective. I reminded him of one of the many things my time in the Corps had taught me: do not worry too much about the things you can't control.

Because life is short. And if nobody's shooting at you, that's one more reason you have to be thankful and content.

43

CIVILIANS CANNOT CARE THE SAME WAY

A common refrain in veteran therapy groups is that civilians have betrayed them by not caring about their combat sacrifices. "We went to war," say veterans, "and they went shopping and put bumper stickers on their cars." Civilians try to respond by thanking veterans for their service, either with sensitivity or bluster. This makes veterans angry, since the profession of thanks implies that civilians are granted absolution from learning about the wars fought on their behalf.

Veterans have a point. Average voters can't tell Karbala from Kandahar, and they certainly don't know about the major battles American warriors fought during the Iraq and Afghanistan wars in both of those cities. When returning vets try to talk about what they did and where they did it, basic geography often restricts empathy. Regular people do not care about Marja, Najaf, Wardak, Ramadi, Kunduz and Tal'Afar. A citizen's ignorance of these places and their significance may seem, to a returning veteran, like questioning Holy Communion's importance to a Catholic.

But can veterans really expect civilians to obsess over the details? They are stressing about mortgages, jobs, kids, dreams, college tuition payments, and, if they're lucky, their life's meaning and purpose. Yes, voters should pay better attention to the places where Americans fight. They should engage politically and own the responsibility of being citizens.

Civilian life, however, has its own challenges. Capitalism demands energy and sweat equity and labor from any profession. All jobs are uncertain in a tough economy. This pummels civilians with constant fear, which they escape by watching the Kardashians make fools of themselves.

Veterans feel this fear too. But veterans have endured deeper fears: death, shame, loss. Sadly, a veteran may scorn civilian escapism, unable to connect with compassion since the civilian didn't fight.

But you volunteered, remember? Go easy on the civilians. They can't care the way you do.

44

MENTORS VS. GUIDES

When I first left the military to write, I made the mistake of measuring my efforts against the accomplishments of people I considered mentors. Had I written a novel? Was I publishing enough opinion pieces? Did I have a new book proposal ready? Was I moving forward like they did?

In the military—as in most bureaucratic structures—mentors are considered important. Career advisors counsel employees to hitch their wagons to a good boss and then rise through the ranks as their guru ascends. But no counselor can answer your most important question: what do you want to do with your life? What brings you meaning?

What will others pay you to accomplish? What is your professional passion? How much risk will you assume to make that passion real?

Eventually, I realized if I wasn't pushing myself to answer these difficult questions for me—and me alone—than any mentor I discovered would be a waste of time. No two successful people ever follow the same paths—nor have any two veterans made their civilian combat time an asset in the same way. Because returning requires self-discovery, depending on nothing more than a mentor's words to tell you how to defeat Exile might short-circuit part of the learning process.

When you befriend an experienced professional in the industry you want to enter, consider them guides, coaches or advisors. Mentorship can creep into hero worship, suggesting you want to grow up to be the same person they are. This outsources your creativity and divine spark, which comes from combining your civilian and combat experiences. It makes the mentor, and not you, accountable for managing your growth. Your best assets, both in transitioning and returning, are your own instincts.

Surround yourself with those who call you out and keep you honest; who challenge your ideas and suggest new possibilities to make your dreams real. But avoid making your life journey their responsibility. Instead, make them guides along the path you choose and take.

45

COMPETE WITH YOURSELF

In the classic 1960 western *The Magnificent Seven*, Yul Brynner's lead rogue character, Chris Adams, tries to describe James Coburn's Britt to the assembling motley crew. He's the best with a gun and a knife, they say, but he has no passion to fight, leaving the group mystified. "If he's the best with a knife and a gun, with whom does he compete?"

"Himself."

Competition matters in tribes and communities. Warriors strive for the highest scores in marksmanship and physical prowess. Academics seek superior grades and strong peer-reviewed commentaries. Stockbrokers and CEOs want higher profit margins. Analysts and marketers measure page views, Facebook likes and re-tweets. Everybody wants data to prove they won the day.

As a transitioning veteran, your metric cannot automatically be fitness scores, fancy titles, or financial portfolios. It can be if you want—there's nothing wrong with that—but that's the point: your metric can be whatever you choose. It may take time to find the thing you're looking for, and you should expect your plan to evolve and change as you grow stronger and more confident in who you are and what you offer your community. Your defeat of Exile will give you an individual warrior's confidence that will be all your own. Mastery is your personal prize.

Comparisons can often create either arrogance (if you believe you're superior to others) or cowardice (if you think you don't measure up). Obsessions with evaluations lead back to Exile, not forward to mastery. Don't measure yourself against anyone else as you pursue your dream.

Instead of comparisons, resolve to compete with yourself and make your best better each day. With a knife or in life, mastery lies in striving for excellence without arrogance, without fear and without a need to prove anything to anyone but you.

46

COMBAT AND ENTREPRENEURSHIP

In early 2012, I spoke with Jim Clifton, the CEO of Gallup, about his book *The Coming Jobs War*. In his book, Clifton convincingly argues that the United States will compete against the world for good jobs throughout the twenty-first century. Unless we're ready to fight for meaningful, valuable work, Clifton says, the American Dream as we know it will no longer exist.

I liked Clifton's pitch and thought the warrior culture offered distinct opportunities for veterans to transition into entrepreneurship. Combat teaches initiative; self-reliance; calculated risk;

determination; positive ambition; selfless loyalty; self-directed action. Successful warriors stake their lives on mixtures of data and instinct, blending Captain Kirk's hunches with Mr. Spock's analyses.

Clifton listened politely but didn't buy it. Gallup had polled veterans for two decades after Vietnam, he said, and all data showed the same result: vets wanted structure, security and uniformity. According to Clifton, the Gallup polling didn't suggest veterans were any better gifted over any other demographic to become entrepreneurs. "Only a very small percentage are even capable of entrepreneurship," Clifton said, "and few of those who are capable ever succeed."

I offered two counterpoints. First, twenty-first century civilian career paths require a much higher level of entrepreneurship than a generation before. A paltry few Americans will retire from the same company where they started out. Most will make self-directed choices and take calculated risks their entire working lives. Second, volunteer veterans are returning to a civilian population that affirms virtue in service. This did not happen after the Vietnam War, when Gallup was polling most veterans.

Although civilians may not always know how to thank veterans for their service, many often try to do the right thing. Veterans can meet them halfway—and perhaps win the jobs war—by setting enthusiastic, entrepreneurial examples as they redefine their civilian identities. If risking your life on your own judgments and hunches wasn't enough to give you original skills, then what is?

47

THE FEAR MONITOR

Napoleon Hill, whose 1937 classic *Think and Grow Rich* helped many Americans reconsider their options and make bold choices during the Great Depression, theorized that all fear manifests itself in six distinct forms: fear of death, old age, the loss of love, ill health, poverty, and/or criticism. What will they think of me if I try to start my own business? What if my family and friends reject me? What if my spouse leaves? What if I fail? How will I survive? Can I bear the tribal shame?

Monitoring fear is important. Sometimes fear's presence is a good sign—it means we're following our true calling and need to stay steady. When I felt fear before a convoy or mission, I took a deep breath before doing my job. I could use fear by letting it go, channeling it to work the problem.

Other times, fear tells us to pay attention. Instincts or intuitions say not to walk down a certain alley, or respond quickly to a certain email, or make a hasty choice. Something we can't explain urges caution. I listen to that too.

Finding balance is the real fight. That is why returning from Exile is a constant struggle. Once you know both war and peace, once you have mastered both worlds, it is up to you entirely to decide which worlds you belong in and at what time. Should I go to war zones where I'm comfortable but endure greater risk? Or spend time in peaceful places, where I'm safer but less productive? Where can I add value? What is best for my family, my friends, my community, and my soul?

Most of the time, acting on our fears is fruitless. But making post-traumatic stress an asset is a continuous fight, so get used to monitoring and not avoiding fear as a regular practice. This is one of many ways combat trauma wards off Exile's presence. Why let the fears of death, loss, or anything else hold you back from your civilian ambitions when you know you've already defeated them before on the battlefield? Just take a deep breath and roll that convoy out.

48

BRILLIANCE IN THE BASICS

A constant Marine Corps combat mantra is "brilliance in the basics." This means one must pay attention to little things as a matter of routine so the bigger issues can be smoothed out and overcome quickly. From marksmanship training to meal rotations, warriors obsess over details so they are able to easily and efficiently make decisions when the enemy threatens.

Every civilian profession demands standards as well, and focusing on the simple basics is as important to the citizen as to the warrior. Keeping your email inbox clean or staying punctual on an appointment schedule may not close the deal, secure the promotion, or land the dream job. But making excellence routine in simple tasks shapes the psychological conditions that move you toward mastery. Identifying the basics you need to be a successful civilian and establishing a pattern of doing them daily is as critical to fighting Exile as a function check of your rifle or field assessment of your gear.

The basics of writing involve words, stories, and ideas. Did I choose the correct phrase? Could I have explained that concept more easily? Did I tell the story so returning veterans and their civilian family and friends can connect intellectually, emotionally and energetically?

As a researcher, the basics are different. Am I paying attention to my surroundings? Am I aware of people's clothing, attitude and shoes? What does their body language indicate? How are they reacting to my presence? What didn't they tell me when I spoke to them? And why?

Professional civilian endeavors of parenting and partnering require fundamentals. Preparing meals, changing diapers, correcting children, communicating interests, maintaining health, increasing fitness, aligning schedules, and deciding vacations all involve standard routines. Become conscious of these processes and deliberately make time to maintain them.

Establish your essentials, and then be brilliant in the basics that your success requires.

49

TIME, MONEY AND ENERGY

War's practical dualities involve attack and defense. What is the proper balance of forces? How quickly must the unit move to seize the center of gravity? Is speed more critical, or will the supply lines become overextended? Are the rear and flanks guarded? Have we rehearsed enough contingencies to be proficient, while also asking creative questions to avoid a complacent routine?

Civilian life is no different. Should I take the easy job that will provide for the family? Can I afford to start that solar panel construction business or invent the new bicycle frame with no financial security? Should I move to New York and join the theater troupe or take the New York Life Insurance job and just volunteer at the community drama center?

In the United States, our epicurean capitalist system grants us control of three resources: time, money and energy. This is the civilian equivalent of war materiel: meals, medicine, water, fuel, ammunition, and spare parts. Pursuing happiness usually involves accumulating as much of these three things as possible and then trading one for the other.

In our jobs, we trade time and energy for money. Then in our personal lives, we trade that money back for material resources that require time and energy to use. We give these resources to children, communities, or anything we choose, and apply fusions of this equation however we see fit.

Controlling and multiplying these resources is never easy. Opposing forces array themselves against your instincts, saying you MUST buy this, you HAVE TO make time for that, you OWE devotion to a person, organization, or union. Often, those voices are Exile's handcuffs.

Be conscious of the trade-offs you make with your time, money and energy. Step back on occasion and reexamine your assumptions and supply lines. Everyone writes their own resource equation, solving for freedom and security in as many different ways as generals attack and defend.

50
TO BE OR TO DO?

In 2008, U.S. Secretary of Defense Robert Gates offered some advice during a speech to a group of senior U.S. Air Force officers. "One day you will take a fork in the road," he said, paraphrasing Air Force Colonel John Boyd. "You can be somebody. You will have to make compromises and turn your back on your friends. But you will be a member of the club and get promoted and get good assignments.

"Or you can do something—something for your country and for yourself. If you decide to do something, you may not get promoted and you may not get good assignments and you certainly will not be a favorite of your superiors. But you won't have to compromise yourself.

"To be somebody or to do something. In life there is often a roll call. That's when you have to make a decision. To be or to do?"

Forget about what it means to "be somebody." It just doesn't matter. Instead, look for opportunities to do valuable things for your community, your country and yourself. No organization, corporation, or client will compensate you to be anything. They will, however, pay you to do something.

As a veteran, do you want to be a victim? Of course not. No man or woman who wears the uniform does so hoping others will pity them for serving. But go one step further—why worry about being anything at all? Instead, consider what you will do in the limited time you have on this earth. What of value can you offer to the world?

And in the process, you may find yourself being somebody anyway. Somebody very important.

You will be You.

51

BECOMING CINCINNATUS

The Roman historian Livy tells the story of Cincinnatus, a wealthy farmer whom the Senate appointed as dictator amidst a national crisis. Hearing of his nomination while tilling his fields, Cincinnatus put his plow aside, fetched his senatorial toga, and accepted his appointment. Sixteen days later he had raised an army and defeated Rome's enemies. Although he held absolute power, Cincinnatus resigned his commission, disbanded his army, and returned to his farm.

I heard the Cincinnatus story at a young age. Like many American boys, I was raised on the classical citizen-soldier ethos and embraced the mythic dream of proving myself as a worthy warrior. Cincinnatus embodied a virtuous ideal. Leaving the plow for a date with destiny and then returning to the farm seemed ethical, honorable and good. Because of this myth, I looked for a field when I left the Marine Corps. If I wanted to be happy again, I had to find some kind of plow.

Those who return today left their own plows for similar reasons that I once did. We responded to a calling; we accepted society's challenge; the tribe's elders told us, in so many ways, they needed us to stand guard, to fight, to kill. We might die, but death seemed a small price to pay in exchange for the rights our fellow citizens possessed to live their lives however they chose. If the Greatest Generation proved themselves worthy by noble deeds in freedom's defense, we also wanted to earn the right to return from something heroic and cultivate our own fields.

So how do we discover which fields to plow? Unlike the early Roman era, the twenty-first century offers little opportunity for a veteran's community to honor the virtue of turning swords into yokes. Cincinnatus fed his family by sluicing soil, planting seeds and reaping the earth's bounty. By contrast, our dreams of twenty-first century information age jobs seem simplistic and shallow. Plowing a field offers clear results, but how can writing and travel put food on the table? You can dream idly about being your own boss, but can you really make a living doing whatever you want?

That intention and purpose was the secret to Cincinnatus' genius. Once the work of war was done—and not a moment longer—he pursued peace with equal vigor and commitment. The humility Cincinnatus displayed when he sent his warriors home and absolved himself of authority suggests his true passions were equally infused with his life on the farm.

The military honors battlefield courage by elevating stories of physical bravery. Men and women who earn Bronze Stars and Medals of Honor respond instantaneously and valiantly to actions that war imposes on them. When the enemy ambushes or the bomb detonates, they kill the attackers and save their wounded comrades. Destroying the threat and rescuing their teammates requires bold determination and courageous initiative.

The Cincinnatus example differentiates between bravery that produces citations and the boldness of pursuing your life's calling. The first requires a response to events out of your control. You can't determine whether the enemy attacks (or, as a civilian, whether the accident, tragedy or death happens), but you respond anyway. The second form of valor, as Cincinnatus shows, requires believing you can achieve an unknown. This is courage of conviction, proactively shaping circumstance with willpower, moving forward with an intention whether others tell you to or not.

Imagine if you held absolute authority over myriad souls. Would you give up command to return to the seasonal uncertainty of a simple plow? Would you send your legions back home instead of keeping them around to do your bidding? Cincinnatus' choice was humble, but it also took guts.

I like to think Cincinnatus fought the war so quickly because he hated the thought of missing that season's harvest. His iron will and unbreakable phalanx may have protected his people, but his life's meaning was in the stuff that fortified his soul: family, fertile land and fulfilling his life's calling. Being Supreme Dictator of Rome may have been cool and all, but it was nothing compared to pruning his vineyards, tending his olive groves, and tilling his farm.

52

REGRETS OF THE DYING

Bronnie Ware, an Australian nurse who spent several years caring for patients in their last twelve weeks, observed that those who wished they could live their lives over again differently all felt common misgivings. In *The Top Five Regrets of the Dying*, Ware tells us the infirm and elderly facing imminent death thought they should have worked less, stayed in closer contact with friends, expressed their honest feelings, and permitted themselves more happiness.

But the number one regret of the dying, Ware says, is not having had the courage to live a life true to their dreams and instead choosing to live the life others expected of them. "When people realize that their life is almost over and look back clearly on it, it is easy to see how many dreams have gone unfulfilled," Ware said in a 2012 interview. "Most people had not honored even half of their dreams, and had to die knowing that it was due to choices they had made or not made."

So how can combat veterans, who dance more closely with death than other civilians, avoid those feelings of failure in their final moments? Jane McGonigal, a game researcher who quoted Ware in a lecture, found building physical, emotional, mental, and social resilience enabled her to overcome depression she suffered after a severe concussion.

Civilians can help veterans find social, mental and emotional resilience through empathy, understanding and affirmation of their warrior identities. Veterans can recognize their warrior comrades previously provided these four resilience structures McGonigal mentions and grow to trust whatever communities they create to support their new place in the civic tribe.

As veterans, we must take charge of our own resilience. We will grow stronger by living our dreams alongside understanding, affirming civilians.

Applying this cycle of awareness will generate growth in both military and civic communities. This decreases the chances that we will be one of Bronnie Ware's bedside casualties whenever we endure our inevitable and Ultimate Return.

53

TO MAKE AND END

I started this book with a quote from T.S. Eliot's *Four Quartets*. When I first read the poem, I thought the middle sentence was a typo; that it was supposed to read "to make an end." In fact, it may have been an error—the quartets have been reprinted in both forms. But through reflecting on the stanza, I discovered a subtle, wise message from the British combat veteran and war poet.

Eliot could have written "end" as a noun. We want our endings to be like this; definite linear things we can hang our hats on. Resolutions. Conclusions. We want our stories to have "the end." But he also knew humans are constantly making and ending; that the terminus of life's journey suggests ongoing creations. That "to make and end" are verbs required to resurrect our spirits and grant our souls a new birth of freedom. An ending is a process, not a period. Life is neither a line nor a circle. It is both.

A friend of mine once observed that no person has a single hero's journey; we are constantly beginning and ending different cycles. In this way, the return from combat is really the commencement of a new adventure; a new challenge; a new level of awareness where mastery in one arena becomes the novice stage of another. The old journey finishes; a new one starts.

When we first come home, Exile's power suffocates our spirits, blanketing our hopes with hatred of civilian life, anger toward epicurean delights, and fear that we will never fit in again. But awareness of war and peace's fundamental truths, appreciation of euphoric and tragic dualities, and application of combat's virtues in routine contexts make us masters of the universal journeys inside our hearts, minds and spirits. Violent demons of death and depression threaten, but vibrant dreams of dynamism and destiny emerge. We engage with the constant struggle to direct combat's mental and emotional energy toward a civilian life that feels more confusing and chaotic every day.

So as we return, and begin, and make, and end, we feel ourselves growing strong in our center. Like stressed vines making wine, the broken places reinforce our resolve and sweeten our spirits. Combat's magic and malevolence never leave us, but we draw on the same places inside us as we move ahead, imagining original opportunities for ourselves and those we love.

In 1865, after the Civil War ended, painter Winslow Homer depicted a Union soldier hunched over a wheat harvest. The man was reaping a field with a scythe, turned away from the rifle, bayonet, canteen, and greatcoat which sat behind him on the ground. The scythe in the painting had not been a harvesting tool for decades; Homer painted the tool as a symbol depicting death. *The Veteran in a New Field*, as the portrait was called, faced away into an unknown future.

When I came back from Iraq, I had not lost a limb or suffered immense brain injury. My jaw gets sore from time to time, but other than that, I'm okay physically. At times I feel the acute confusion, anger and loneliness of Exile, but other than that, I'm okay emotionally. In the decade since I left the Marines, I failed several times at writing, business and life—but those challenges provided lessons that became the grist for future goals.

When I left the Marine Corps, I had an intention to find my farm and plow. And you do too, or else you wouldn't have read this far. Like the Union soldier in Winslow Homer's painting and like Odysseus in ancient Homer's great book, you have made and ended your war.

Now it is your turn. Teach us how to make war meaningful in peace. Show us how to ascend to mastery. The end is where you begin fighting Exile. And we can't wait to watch you win.

ACKNOWLEDGMENTS

Grateful thanks to Mike Lehnert, Chris Neese, Jim Mattis, Charity Winters, Jason Howell, Nate Fick, Mike Noonan, Robin Bhatty, Mac Owens, Jamie Cox, Scott Mann, Rodger Schneidau, Benn Danelo, Ted Grubbs, and Luke Tatro, who—as combat veterans on their own returns—guided, sculpted and affirmed this material in more conversations and ways than I can count.

To Batya Rotter, Eugenia Lee, Megan Hannan, Robin Rice, Eileen Guo, Allan Gerson, Matt Furey, and my mother Kathy Danelo, who shared compassionate and insightful civilian observations.

To Tim Feist, Steve Le, and my father Dan Danelo, military veterans who did not deploy in combat, yet offered invaluable perspective from their own transitions and returns.

To Steve Pressfield and Shawn Coyne, for validating, challenging, editing, and publishing. To Luke Bienstock, for exceptional interning.

To Vidya, for partnership and love. To Suvali and Rumita, for inspiration and wonder.

And to Istanbul: the place that masters dueling worlds, and where I discovered the extent of the magic.

ABOUT THE AUTHOR

 **David J. Danelo** writes about international affairs, directs field research for the Foreign Policy Research Institute, and consults independently on international border management.

Danelo graduated from the U.S. Naval Academy in 1998 and served seven years as an infantry officer in the Marine Corps. In 2004, Captain Danelo served near Fallujah with the First Marine Expeditionary Force as a convoy commander, intelligence officer and provisional executive officer for a rifle company.

Danelo is also the author of *Blood Stripes: The Grunt's View of the War in Iraq* and *The Border: Exploring the U.S.-Mexican Divide*, both of which received awards from the Military Writers Society of America.